A Note to Parents and Caregivers:

Read-it! Joke Books are for children who are moving ahead on the amazing road to reading. These fun books support the acquisition and extension of reading skills as well as a love of books.

Published by the same company that produces *Read-it!* Readers, these books introduce the question/answer and dialogue patterns that help children expand their thinking about language structure and book formats.

When sharing joke books with a child, read in short stretches. Pause often to talk about the meaning of the jokes. The question/answer and dialogue formats work well for this purpose and provide an opportunity to talk about the language and meaning of the jokes. Have the child turn the pages and point to the pictures and familiar words. When you read the jokes, have fun creating the voices of characters or emphasizing some important words. Be sure to reread favorite jokes.

There is no right or wrong way to share books with children. Find time to read with your child, and pass on the legacy of literacy.

Adria F. Klein, Ph.D.
Professor Emeritus
California State University
San Bernardino, California

Managing Editors: Bob Temple, Catherine Neitge
Creative Director: Terri Foley
Editors: Jerry Ruff, Christianne Jones
Designer: Les Tranby
Page production: Picture Window Books
The illustrations in this book were rendered electronically.

Picture Window Books
5115 Excelsior Boulevard
Suite 232
Minneapolis, MN 55416
877-845-8392
www.picturewindowbooks.com

Printed in the United States of America.

Library of Congress Cataloging-in-Publication Data
Dahl, Michael.
Roaring with laughter : a book of animal jokes / by Michael Dahl ;
illustrated by Anne Haberstroh.
p. cm. — (Read-it! joke books—supercharged!)
ISBN 1-4048-0628-8
1. Animals—Juvenile humor. 2. Wit and humor, Juvenile.
I. Title. II. Series.

PN6231.A5D36 2004
818'.5402—dc22   2004007324

Roaring with Laughter

A Book of Animal Jokes

By Michael Dahl • Illustrated by Anne Haberstroh

Reading Advisers:
Adria F. Klein, Ph.D.
Professor Emeritus, California State University
San Bernardino, California

Susan Kesselring, M.A., Literacy Educator
Rosemount-Apple Valley-Eagan (Minnesota) School District

What do you get when you cross a duck with an alligator?

A quack-odile.

Where did the cow go
on the weekend?

To the mooovies.

Why did the caterpillar get sick?

*There was a bug
going around.*

What do you get when you put
a turkey in the freezer?

A brrrrrrrd.

What holiday do wolves
celebrate in the fall?

Howl – oween!

Why did the pelican get kicked
out of the hotel?

It had a big bill.

Why did the bee trip
over the flower?

It was a stumble-bee.

What does a cow read in
the morning?

The moospaper.

What do you get if you cross
a bumblebee with a doorbell?
A hum-dinger!

Why did the snowman call
his watchdog Frost?
Because Frost bites!

What time is it when an
elephant sits on a fence?
Time to fix the fence!

What do polar bears
eat for lunch?

Icebergers.

What's big and gray and has
lots of horns?

An elephant marching band.

How did the little fish get
to school?

It took the octobus.

What kind of snake is good at
cleaning cars?

A windshield viper.

What do you call a camel
at the North Pole?

Lost!

What is the biggest ant in
the world?

An eleph-ant.

What kind of ant is good
at math?

An account-ant.

What goes "hum-choo! hum-choo!"?

A bee with a cold.

What do chickens do on Valentine's Day?

They give each other pecks.

What did one bee say to the other bee on a hot summer day?

"Sure is swarm, isn't it?"

What did the pony say when it had a sore throat?

"Sorry, but I'm a little horse."

What goes "zzub zzub"?

A bee flying backwards.

Why did the skunk become
a general in the army?

It was good at giving odors.

What follows a lion wherever
it goes?

Its tail.

How did the rabbits survive
the car crash?

The car had hare bags.

Why did the squirrel go
crazy in the winter?

*Because her nest
was full of nuts!*

What clothes do skydiving
rabbits like to wear?

Jumpsuits.

What do you call a crate
full of ducks?

A box of quackers.

Why did the mole dig a tunnel
into the bank?

To burrow some money.

How do rich birds make
their money?

They invest in the

stork market!

Why do turkeys always
lose at baseball?

They can only hit fowl balls.

What kind of lions live in
your front yard?

Dande-lions.

15

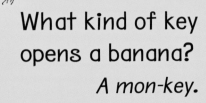

What kind of key
opens a banana?

A mon-key.

What did the little centipede
say to its mother when they
went shopping?

*"I need a new pair of shoes.
And a new pair of shoes."*

Why was the rooster
all wet?

*He was covered with
cock-a-doodle dew.*

What did the duck say when she
bought some lipstick?

"Put it on my bill."

What do you call a chicken
that likes to eat cement?

A brick layer.

What do you call a crazy chicken?

A cuckoo cluck.

How did the grizzly
catch a cold?

He walked outside with
just his bear feet.

What did the cow ride when
her car broke down?

A moo-torcycle.

What do chickens eat at
birthday parties?

       Coop cakes.

Where do cows go in a
rocket ship?

       To the mooooon.

What do rabbits use to make
their ears look nice?

       Hare spray.

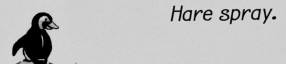

What do bees wear when they go to work?

Buzz-ness suits.

When dolphins play football, how do they know which team gets the ball?

They flip for it.

Why do mother kangaroos hate rainy days?

Because the kids have to play inside.

What kind of airplane do elephants ride in?

Jumbo jets.

Why don't animals play cards in the jungle?

Too many cheetahs.

Why do birds fly south
in the winter?
>It's too far to walk.

What is the best kind of
computer bug?
>A spider. They make
>the best Web sites.

What do sharks put on their
toast for breakfast?
>Jellyfish.

Why did the crow perch
on the telephone wire?

>*He was going to make
a long-distance caw.*

How did the flea travel
from dog to dog?
>*It went itch-hiking.*

Where do polar bears
keep their money?
>*In a snowbank.*

Look for all of the books in this series:

Read-it! Joke Books—Supercharged!

Beastly Laughs
A Book of Monster Jokes

Chalkboard Chuckles
A Book of Classroom Jokes

Creepy Crawlers
A Book of Bug Jokes

Roaring with Laughter
A Book of Animal Jokes

Sit! Stay! Laugh!
A Book of Pet Jokes

Spooky Sillies
A Book of Ghost Jokes

Read-it! Joke Books

Alphabet Soup
A Book of Riddles About Letters

Animal Quack-Ups
Foolish and Funny Jokes About Animals

Bell Buzzers
A Book of Knock-Knock Jokes

Chewy Chuckles
Deliciously Funny Jokes About Food

Crazy Criss-Cross
A Book of Mixed-Up Riddles

Ding Dong
A Book of Knock-Knock Jokes

Dino Rib Ticklers
Hugely Funny Jokes About Dinosaurs

Doctor, Doctor
A Book of Doctor Jokes

Door Knockers
A Book of Knock-Knock Jokes

Family Funnies
A Book of Family Jokes

Funny Talk
A Book of Silly Riddles

Galactic Giggles
Far-Out and Funny Jokes About Outer Space

Laughs on a Leash
A Book of Pet Jokes

Monster Laughs
Frightfully Funny Jokes About Monsters

Nutty Neighbors
A Book of Knock-Knock Jokes

Open Up and Laugh!
A Book of Knock-Knock Jokes

Rhyme Time
A Book of Rhyming Riddles

School Buzz
Classy and Funny Jokes About School

School Daze
A Book of Riddles About School

Teacher Says
A Book of Teacher Jokes

Three-Alarm Jokes
A Book of Firefighter Jokes

Under Arrest
A Book of Police Jokes

Who's There?
A Book of Knock-Knock Jokes

Zoodles
A Book of Riddles About Animals